Reasoning and Writing

Level B
Workbook 2

Siegfried Engelmann

Ann Brown Arbogast

Karen Lou Seitz Davis

A Division of The McGraw-Hill Companies

Columbus, Ohio

Cover Credits

(t) Photo Spin, (b) PhotoDisc.

SRA/McGraw-Hill

A Division of The McGraw·Hill Companies

2008 Imprint
Copyright © 2001 by SRA/McGraw-Hill.

Send all inquiries to:
SRA/McGraw-Hill
4400 Easton Commons
Columbus, OH 43219

Printed in the United States of America.

ISBN 0-02-684761-2

18 19 20 21 HES 17 16 15 14

Lesson 36

A.

B.

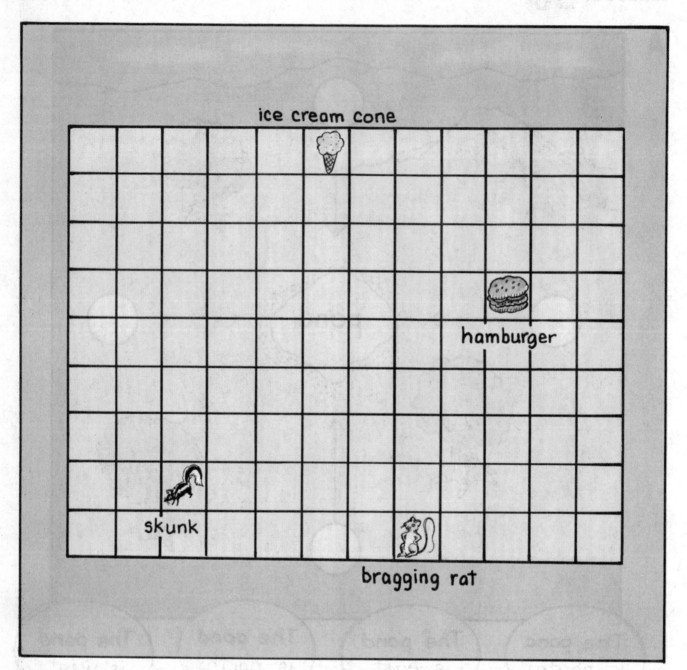

Step A.   4 squares north

Step B.   3 squares west

Step C.   4 squares north

Step D.   2 squares west

Step E.   7 squares south

The bragging rat ended up at the _____ .

C.

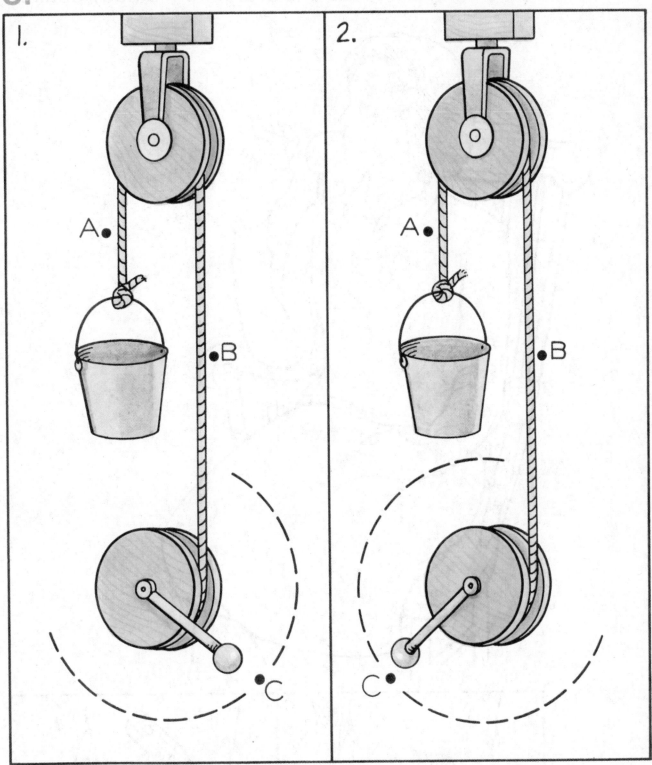

1.

2.

D. Mother held Baby Sarah as she drank from a baby bottle.

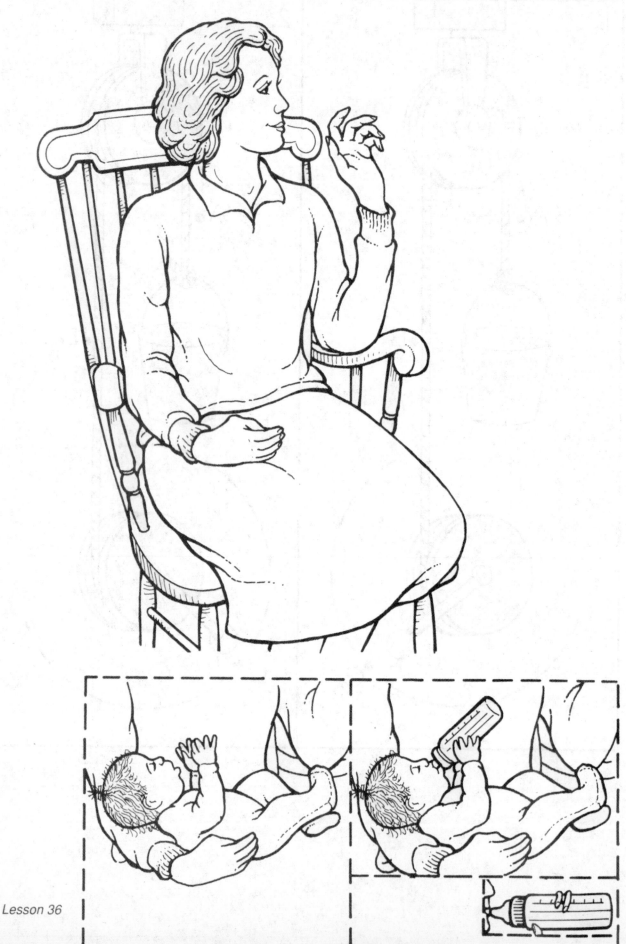

Lesson 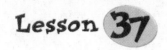 37

A.

rat

hot dog

beehive

skunk

apple

Step A.   3 squares north

Step B.   1 square east

Step C.   1 square south

Step D.   3 squares west

Step E.   4 squares north

The skunk ended up at the _____ .

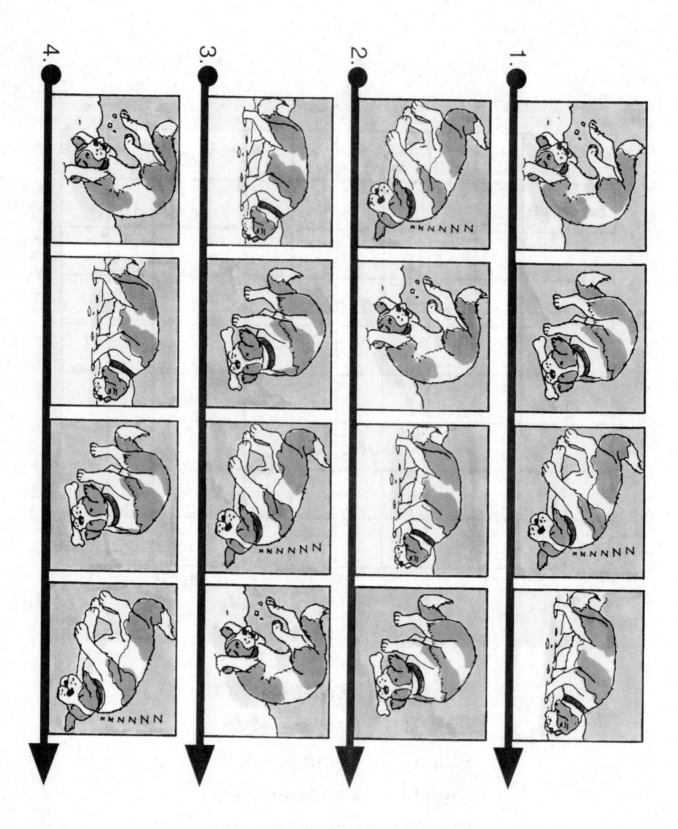

C.

1. Our car made a dust cloud. It floated away.

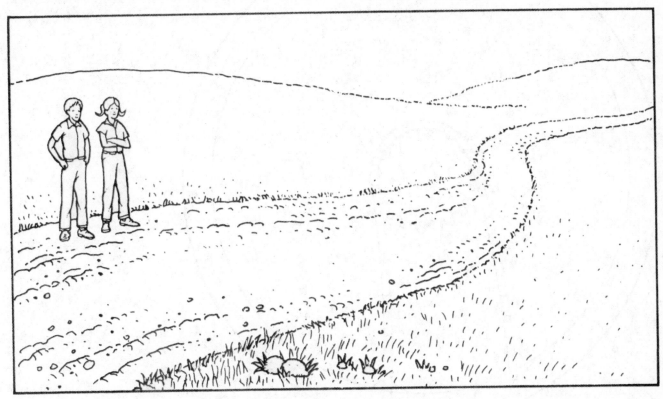

2. A frog was on top of the car. It had big black spots all over.

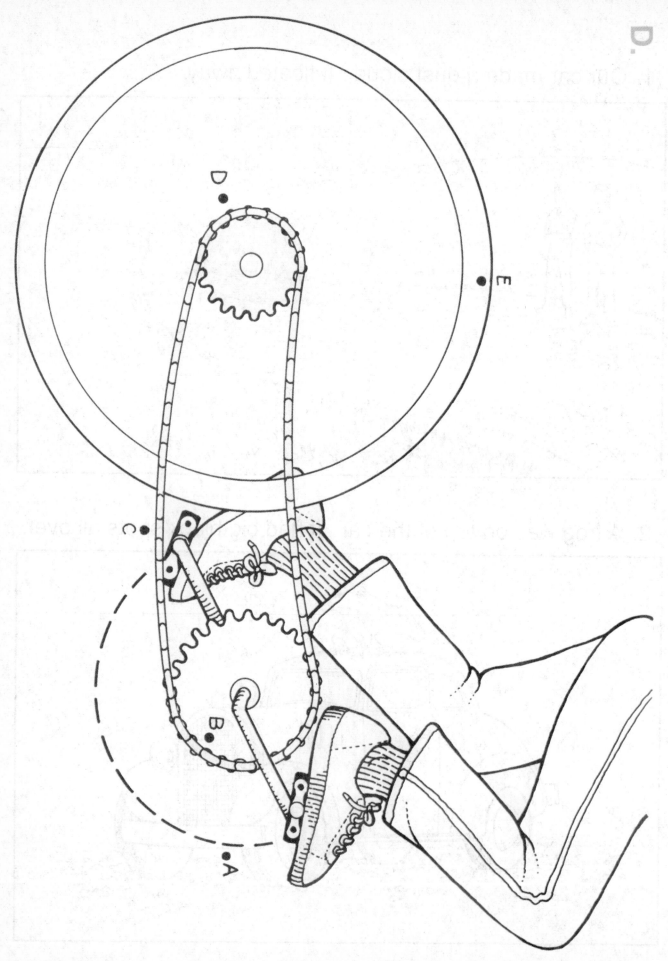

Lesson 38

A.

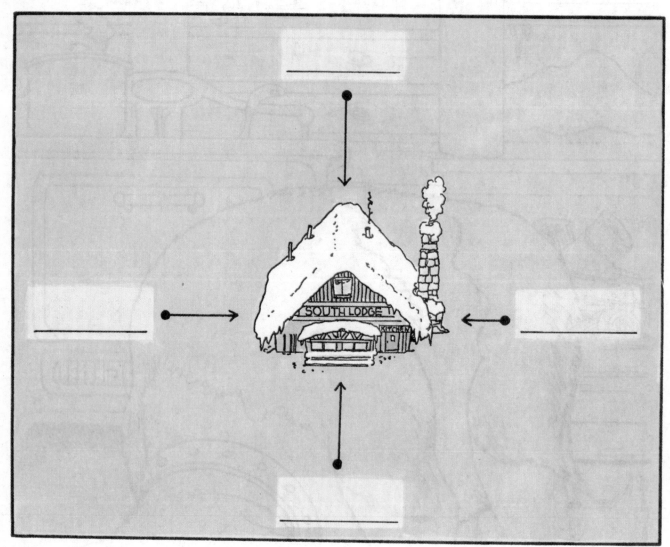

Zelda

Bleep

Dot

Molly

B.

We had a fence next to the barn. Our dog jumped over it.

C.

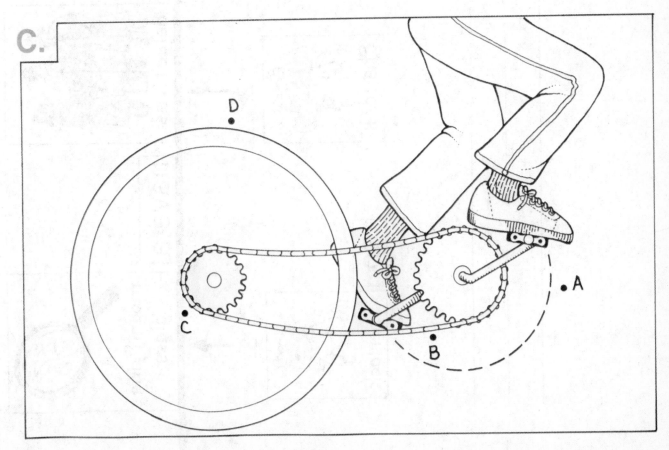

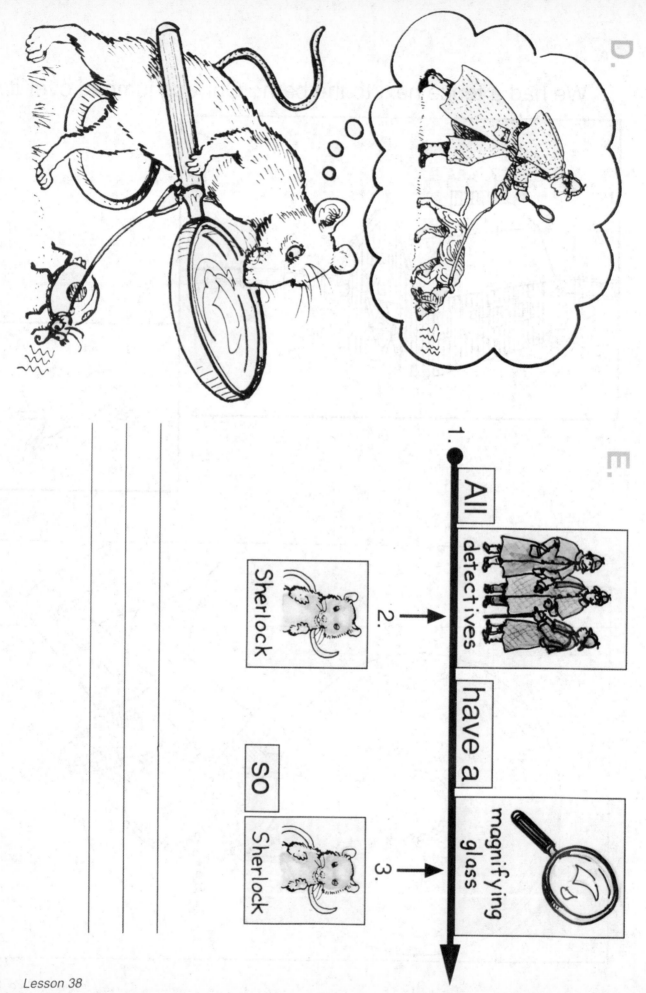

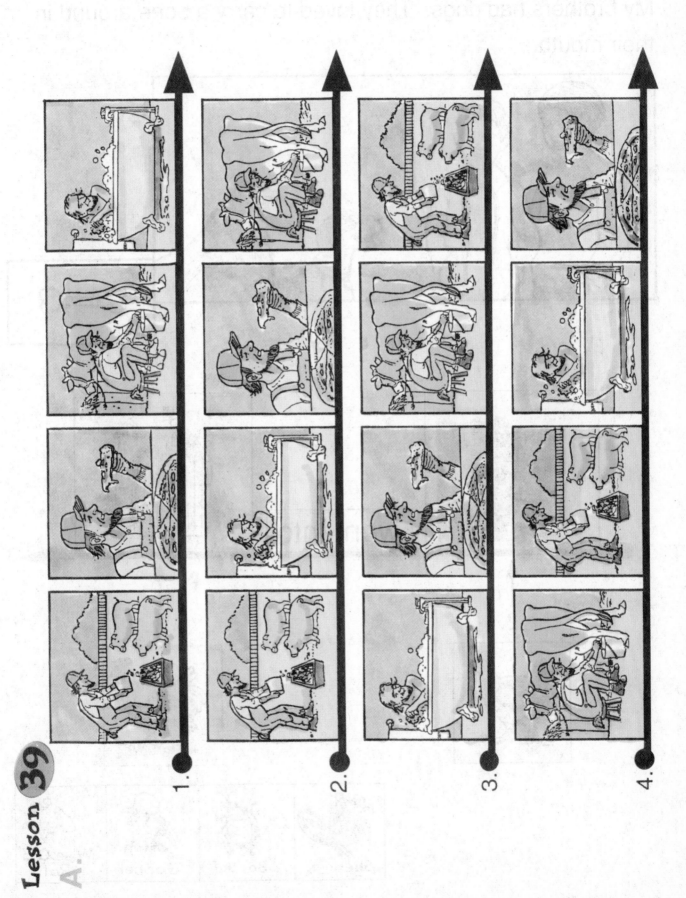

1.

2.

3.

4.

B.

My brothers had dogs. They loved to carry a bone around in their mouth.

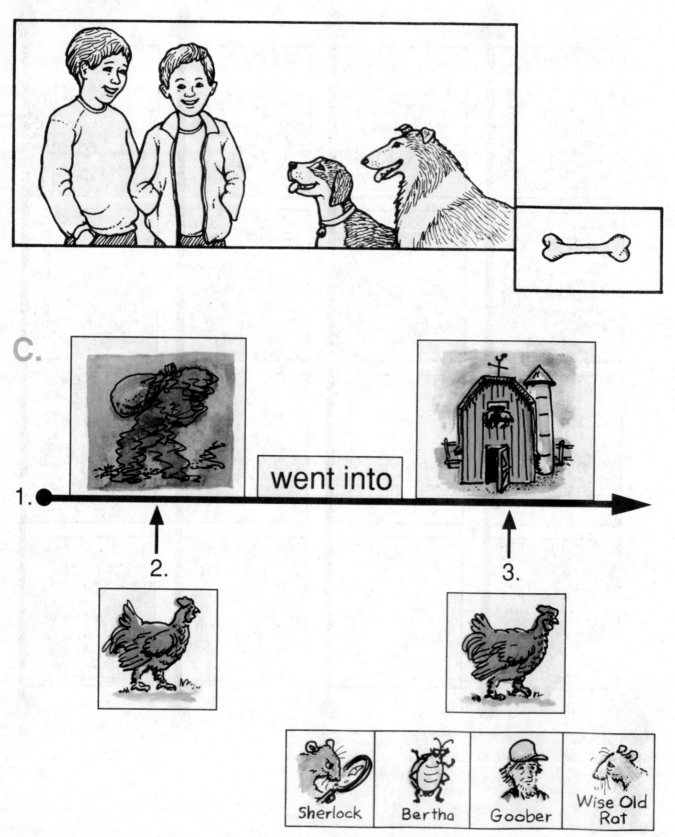

C.

went into

1.
2.
3.

Sherlock   Bertha   Goober   Wise Old Rat

A.

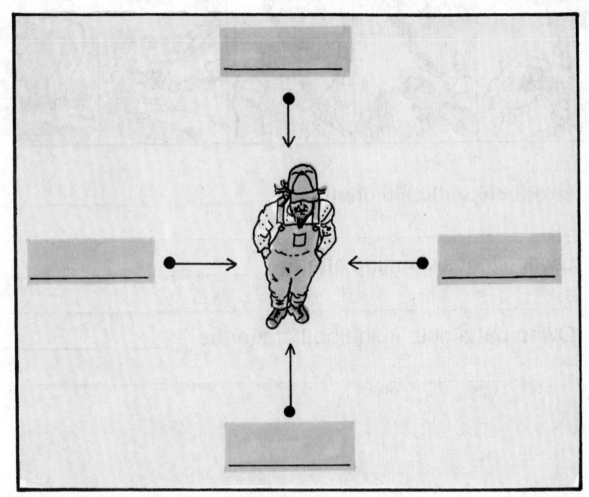

Goober is north. — Dud

Goober is west. — Ranger

Goober is south. — Bleep

B.

1. Owen ate bananas after he _____

_____.

2. Owen went swimming after he _____

_____.

3. Owen put a note in the bottle after he _____

_____.

C.

1. boys   children
2. animals   cows
3. fruit   apples

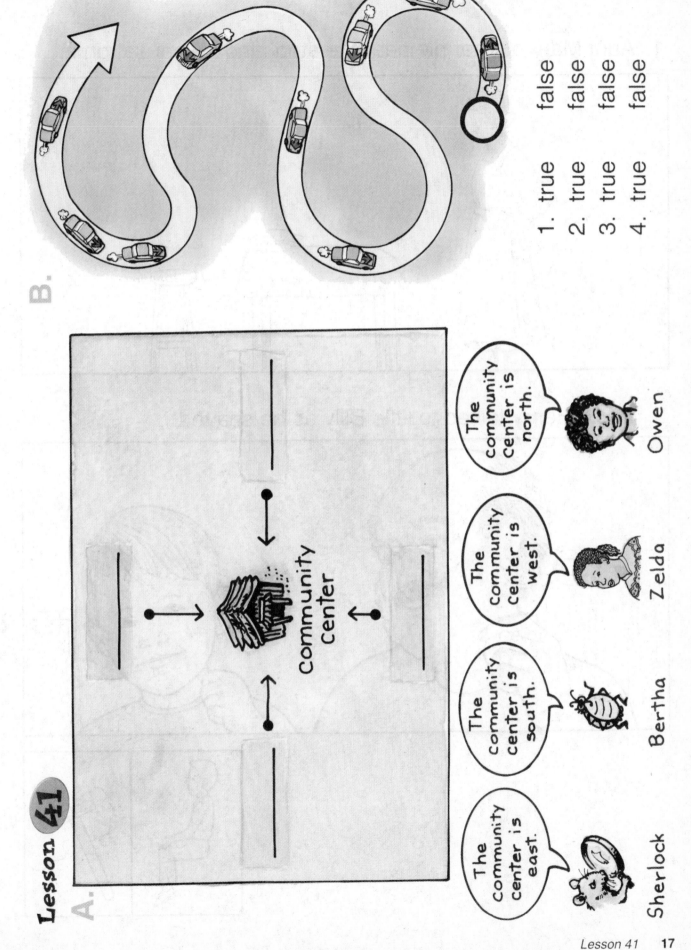

C.

1. Aunt Mary put her pie near the stool and Wilber sat on it.

2. Uncle Henry talked to little Billy as he shaved.

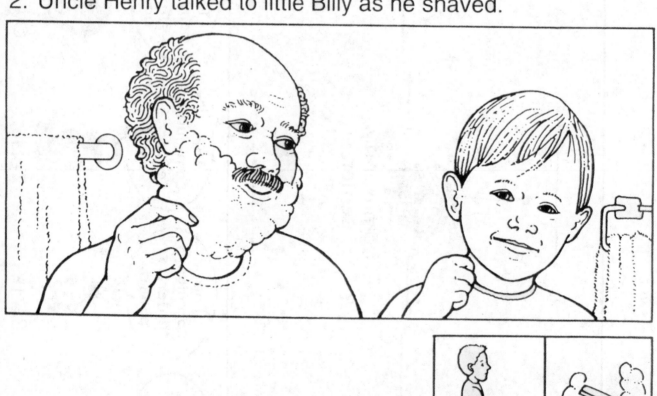

D.

Lesson 42

A.

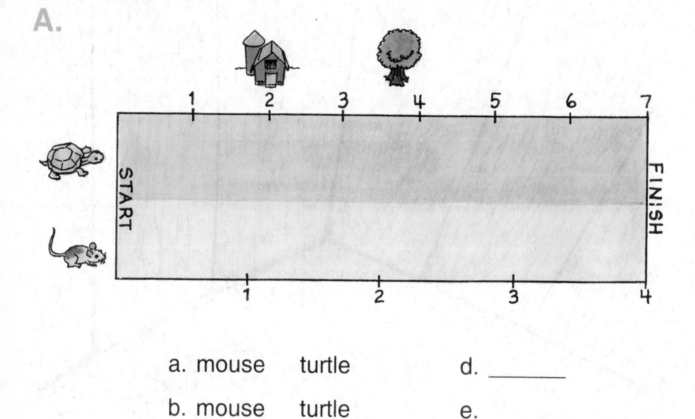

a. mouse   turtle   d. _____

b. mouse   turtle   e. _____

c. mouse   turtle

B.

When the boys petted the dogs, they wagged their tails.

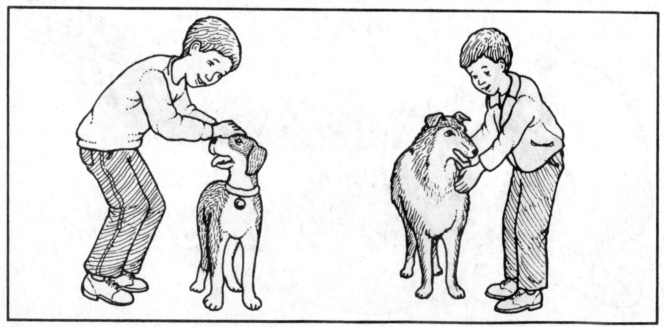

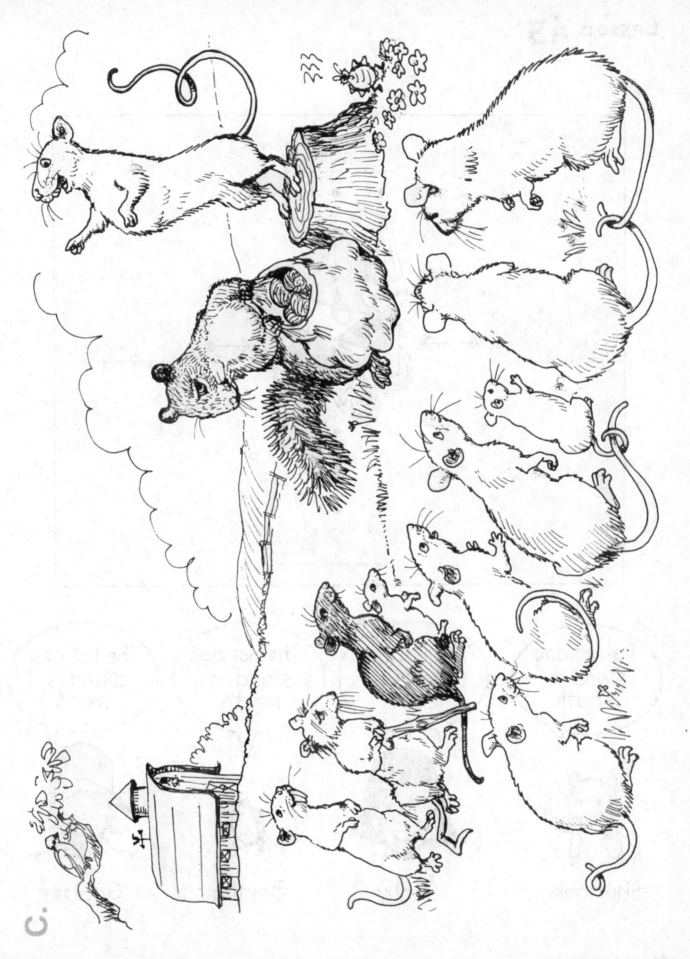

C.

A.

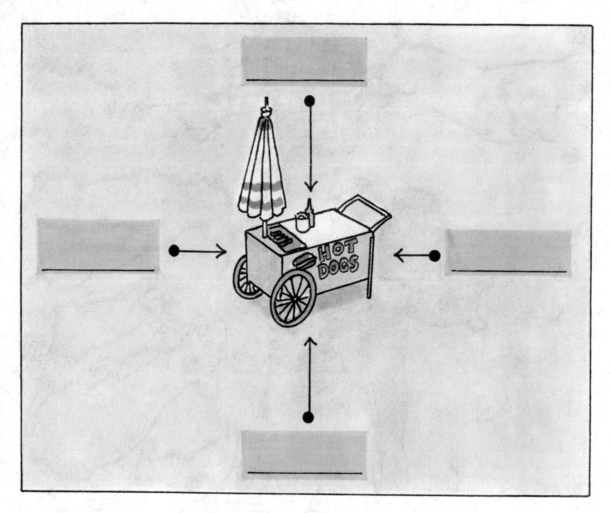

B.

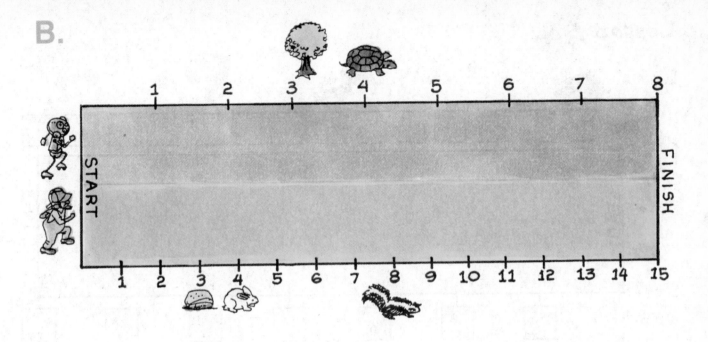

a. Bleep   Goober   d. _____

b. Bleep   Goober   e. _____

c. Bleep   Goober   f. _____

C.

The children caught butterflies. They had orange wings.

Lesson 44

A.

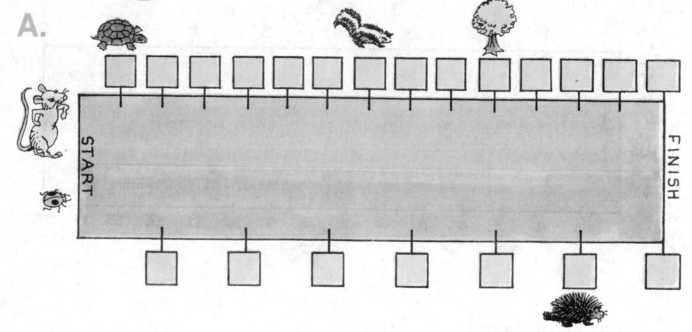

a. Sherlock	Bertha	d. _____
b. Sherlock	Bertha	e. _____
c. Sherlock	Bertha	f. _____

B.

Where is Fred the frog in the afternoon?

a. In the afternoon, all the _____ are on lily pads.

b. Fred is a _____.

c. So in the afternoon, _____.

C.

went swimming	stood on a stump
Sherlock	Zelda
painted a picture	Bertha

1. _____

2. _____

3. _____

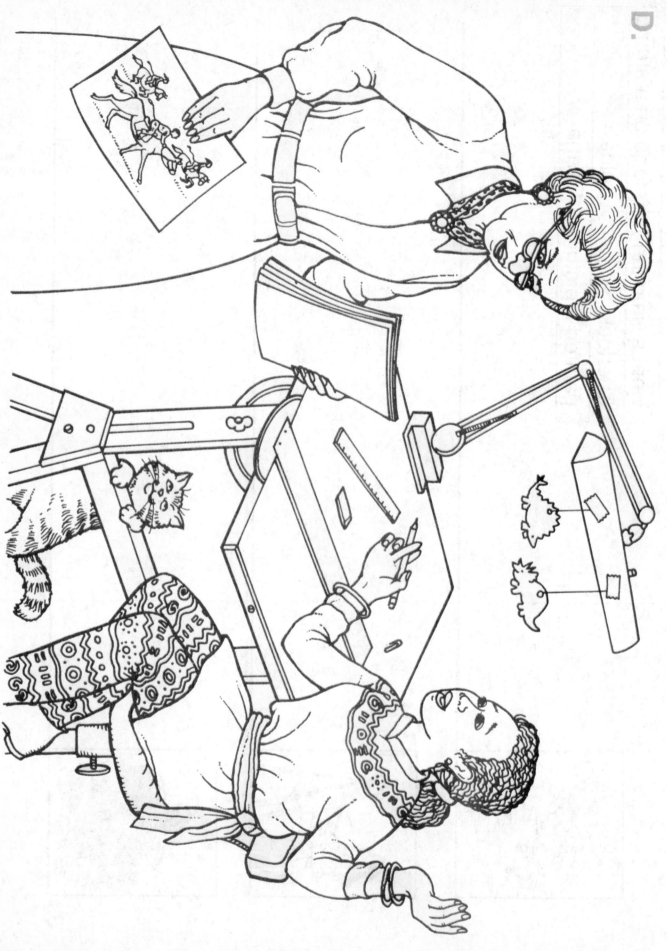

Lesson 45

A.

Goober	Paul
painted a pot	fed the pigs
sat on an apple	Fizz and Liz

1.

2.

3.

B.

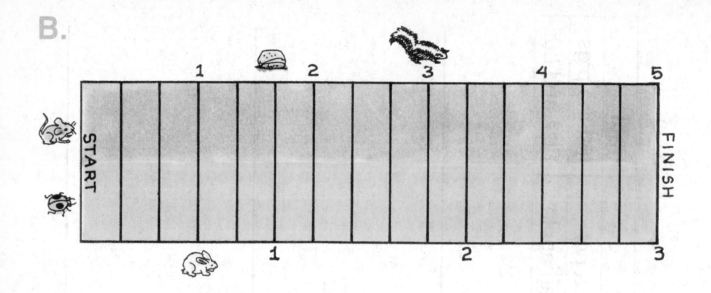

a. mouse   Bertha   d. _____

b. mouse   Bertha   e. _____

c. mouse   Bertha   f. _____

C.

The girls had pet goats. One of them had very long horns.

D.

Where is Sherlock after dinner?

barn

1. After dinner, all the rats are _____.
2. Sherlock _____.
3. So after dinner, _____.

Lesson 46

A.

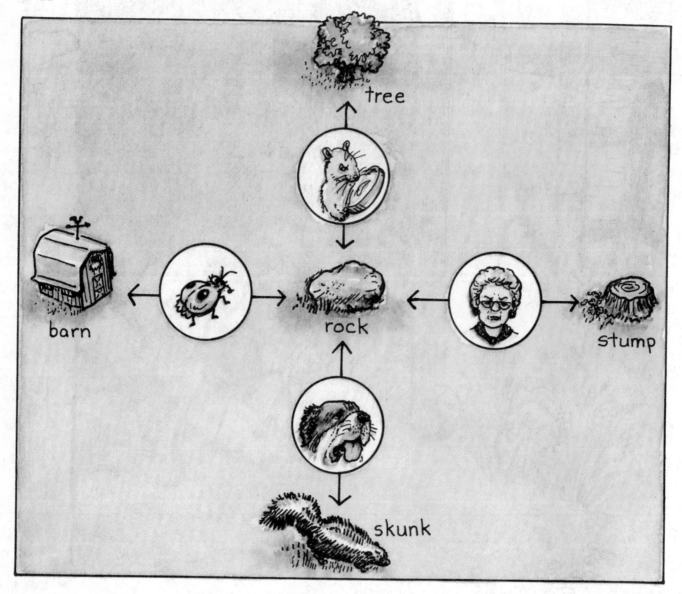

1. Bertha said, "The rock is _____ of me and the
   _____ is _____ of me."

2. Mrs. Hudson said, "The rock is _____ of me
   and the _____ is _____ of me."

3. Sherlock said, "The rock is _____ of me and
   the _____ is _____ of me."

played in the snow
kissed Bleep
painted a paddle

B.

1. 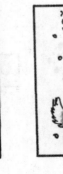 _____

2.  _____

3.  _____

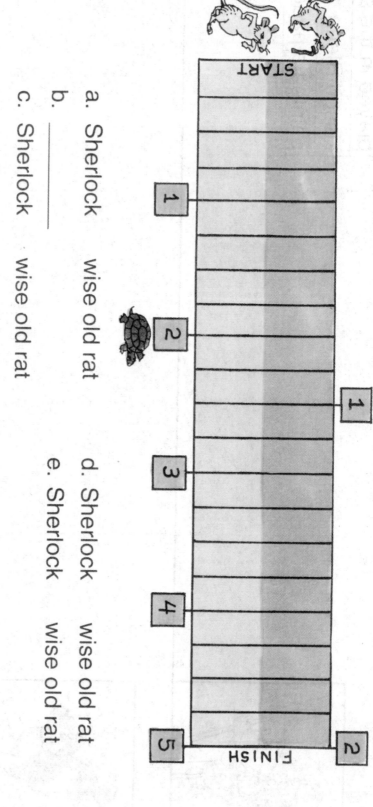

a. Sherlock   wise old rat

b. _____

c. Sherlock   wise old rat

d. Sherlock   wise old rat

e. Sherlock   wise old rat

It's very difficult to understand.

A.

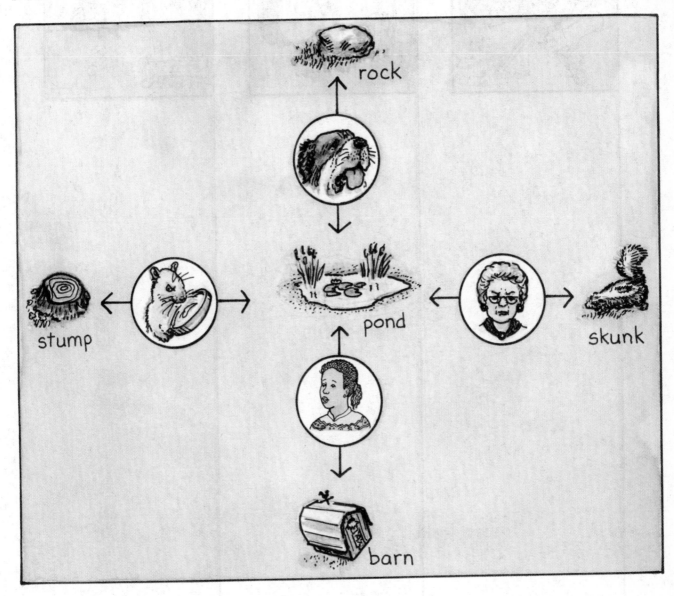

1. Zelda said, "The pond is _____ of me and the _____ is _____ of me."

2. Sherlock said, "The pond is _____ of me and the _____ is _____ of me."

3. Mrs. Hudson said, "The pond is _____ of me and the _____ is _____ of me."

B.

1.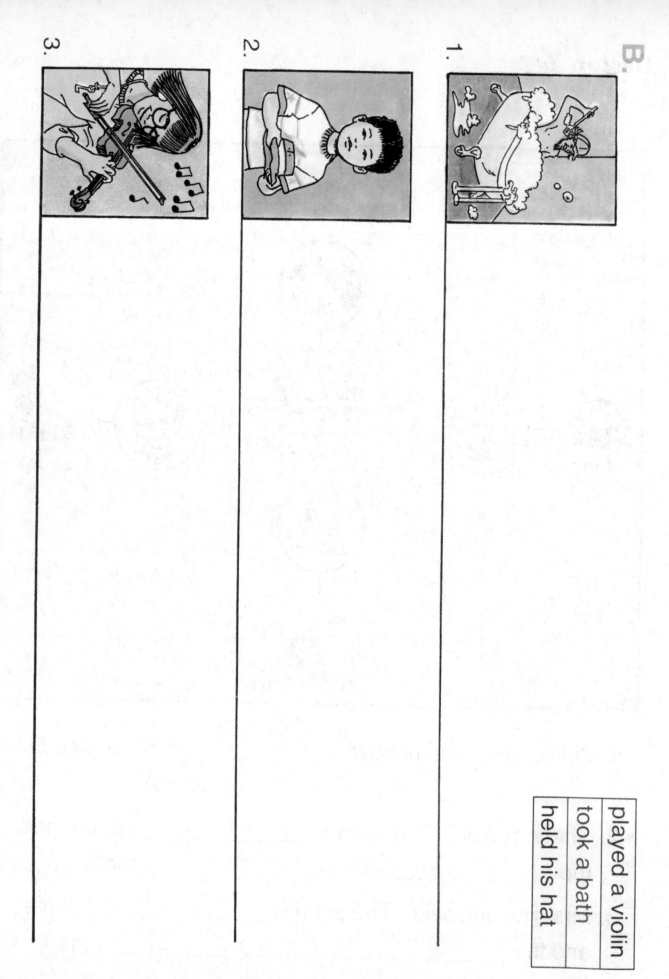

2.

3.

| played a violin |
| took a bath |
| held his hat |

C.

1. The boys played with dogs. The dogs had short tails.

2. The girls went in boats. The boats were made of wood.

3. The truck went up a hill. The truck had a flat tire.

A.

a. skunk   Bertha
b. ___
c. skunk   Bertha
d. skunk   Bertha
e. skunk   Bertha
f. ___

B.

Bleep	rolled in the mud
Dud	sat on Roger
Zelda	played in the snow
Mrs. Hudson	chased a skunk
	said silly things

1. _____

2. _____

3. _____

Lesson 49

A.

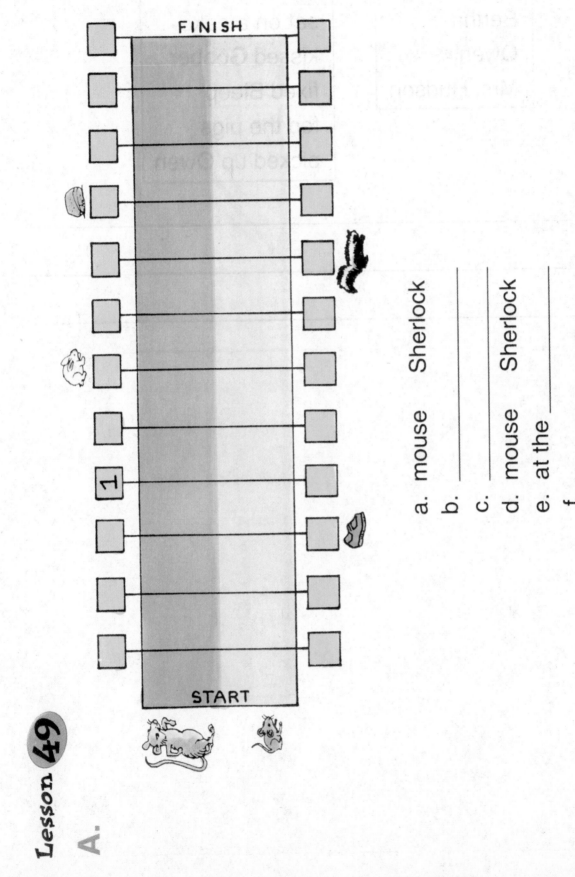

FINISH

START

a. mouse Sherlock

b. _____

c. _____

d. mouse Sherlock

e. at the _____

f. _____

g. _____

B.

Molly	ran home
Bertha	sat on a cake
Owen	kissed Goober
Mrs. Hudson	fixed Bleep
	fed the pigs
	picked up Owen

1. _____

2. _____

3. _____

C.

Lesson 50 – Test 5

A.

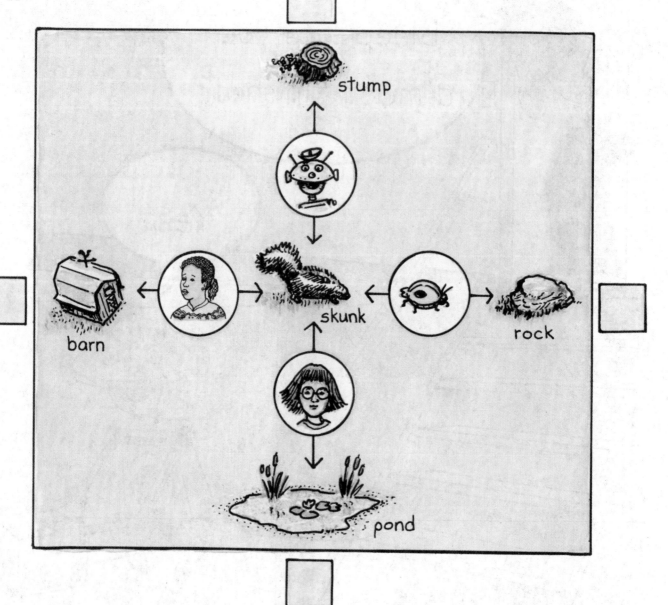

1. Zelda said, "The skunk is _____ of me and the
_____ is _____ of me."

2. Molly said, "The skunk is _____ of me and the
_____ is _____ of me."

3. Bertha said, "The skunk is _____ of me and
the _____ is _____ of me."

B.

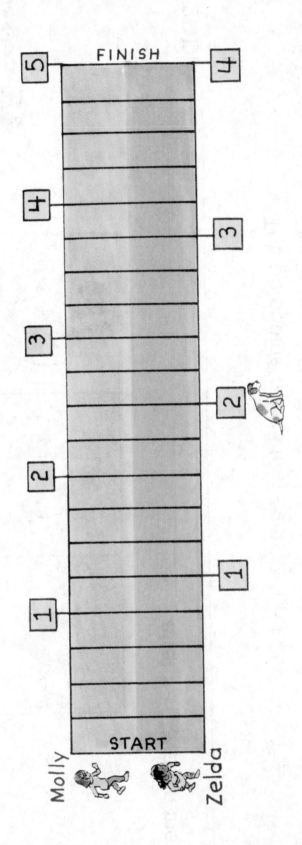

a. Molly   Zelda

b. _____

c. Molly   Zelda

d. Molly   Zelda

e. Molly   Zelda

A.

1. _____

2. Dud _____ after he played in the snow.

B.

The porcupine runs 5 feet each second.
The mouse runs 3 feet each second.

START

FINISH

a. _____

b. _____

c. mouse   porcupine

d. _____

e. _____

C.

1. Aunt Martha pulled a turnip out of the dirt.

   The turnip tasted good.

2. The ranger led the dogs toward the mountains.

   The mountains were covered with snow.

Lesson 52

A.

1. _____

2. _____

B.

FINISH

The wise old rat runs 10 feet each second.
The toy car goes 2 feet each second.

START

a. _____   b. _____   c. wise old rat   toy car   d. _____

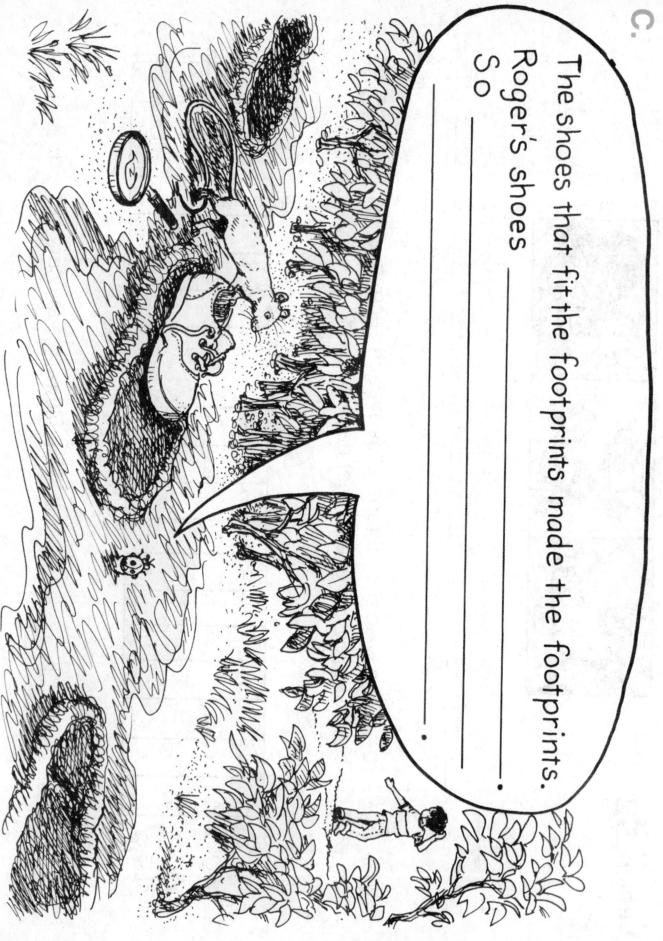

C.

The shoes that fit the footprints made the footprints.

Roger's shoes _____

So _____
_____ .
_____ .

Lesson 53

A.

1. _____

2. _____

B.

The woolly worm goes 3 inches each second.

The spider goes 2 inches each second.

FINISH

START

a. _____ b. _____ c. woolly worm d. _____ e. _____

spider

C.

The shoes that smell of squash went in squash.

Goober's shoes _____

So _____

D.

A.

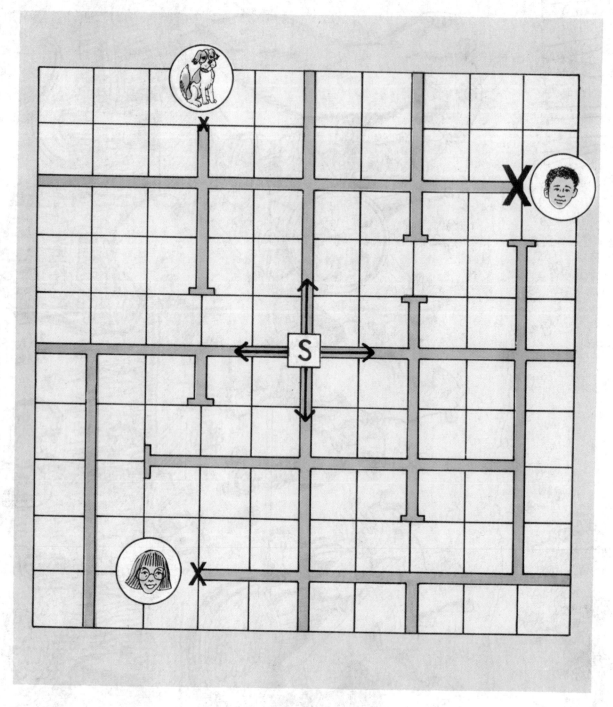

1. To go to Molly, you go _____ miles _____ and _____ miles _____ .

2. To go to Owen, you go _____ miles _____ and _____ miles _____ .

B.

1. Three ladies picked berries.

   The berries were blue.

2. Our chicken laid an egg.

   The egg was no bigger than a stone.

3. We used a shovel to plant the flower.

   The flower grew all summer long.

C.

The wise old rat goes 10 feet each second.

The mouse goes 3 feet each second.

FINISH

a. _____ b. _____ c. _____ d. _____

Lesson 55

A.

1. To go to Bleep, you go ____ miles ____ and ____ miles ____.

2. To go to Owen, you go ____ miles ____ and ____ miles ____.

B.

The porcupine goes 5 feet each second.
The mouse goes 4 feet each second.

a. ____

b. ____

c. ____

d. at the ____

e. ____

FINISH

C.

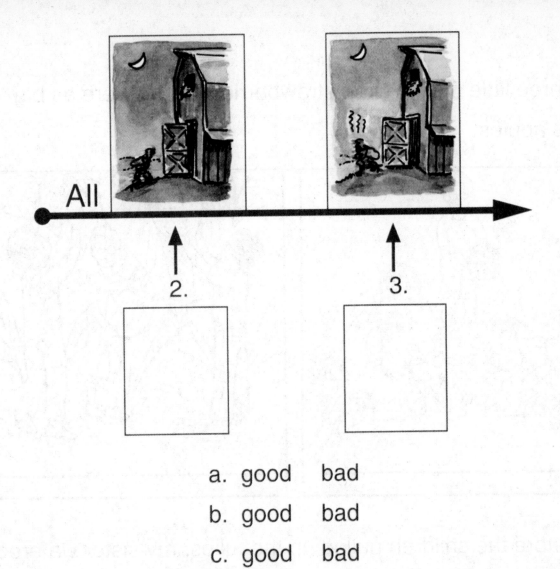

a. good   bad

b. good   bad

c. good   bad

D.

All characters who go into the barn smell of oats.

Molly _____

_____

E.

1. Three little boys picked strawberries. They were as big as apples.

2. Before the children pulled up the tulips, my sister watered them with the hose.

Lesson 56

A.

1.

2.

3.

1. _____

_____

2. _____

_____

B.

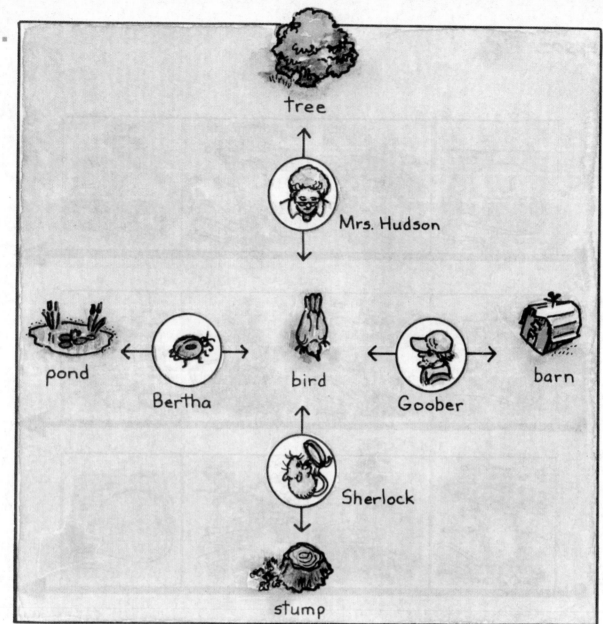

1. _____ said, "The bird is _____ of me and the _____ is _____ of me."

2. _____ said, "The bird is _____ of me and the _____ is _____ of me."

3. _____ said, "The bird is _____ of me and the _____ is _____ of me."

C.

1. Zelda drove a van to the picnic.   reports   does not report

2. Three people sat at a picnic table.   reports   does not report

3. Everybody was going to swim later that day.   reports   does not report

4. Roger wore a hat.   reports   does not report

5. Zelda ate more than anybody else.   reports   does not report

6. A van was close to the picnic table.   reports   does not report

7. Zelda sat next to Mrs. Hudson.   reports   does not report

D.

Donna and her mother watched the tiny spiders. They were upside down in their web.

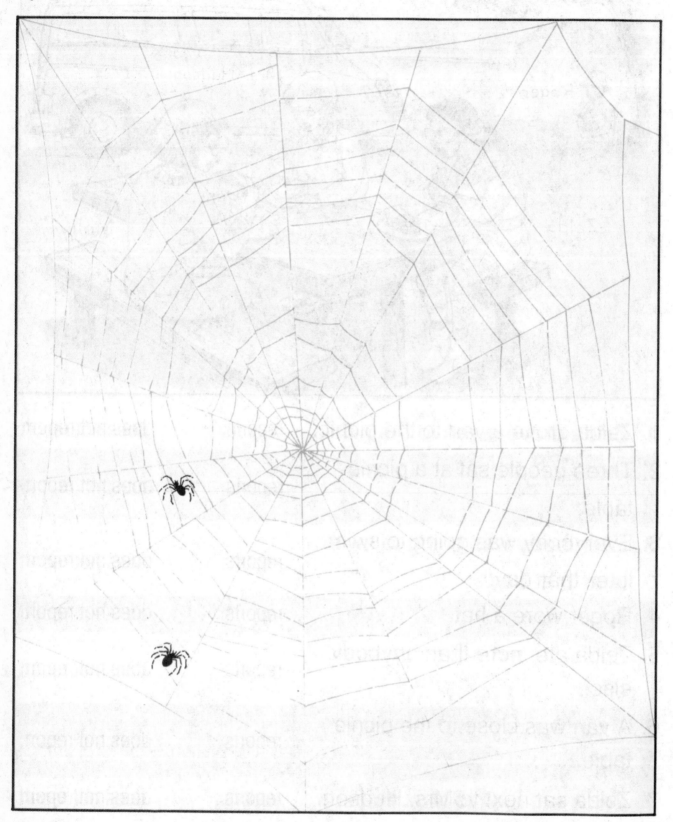

Lesson 57

A.

1. Sherlock ate too much corn.	reports	does not report
2. Bertha was mad at Sherlock.	reports	does not report
3. Cyrus pulled a large sack.	reports	does not report
4. Bertha played a violin.	reports	does not report
5. The wise old rat was dirty.	reports	does not report
6. The sack was full of hazelnuts.	reports	does not report
7. The wise old rat was wet.	reports	does not report

B.

ate a burger
sat under a tree
drove a van
went fishing
ate watermelon
sat on a table
ate pie

C.

1. This lamp goes in the bag.

2. I ran on the track.

3. The stamps are in a stack.

D.

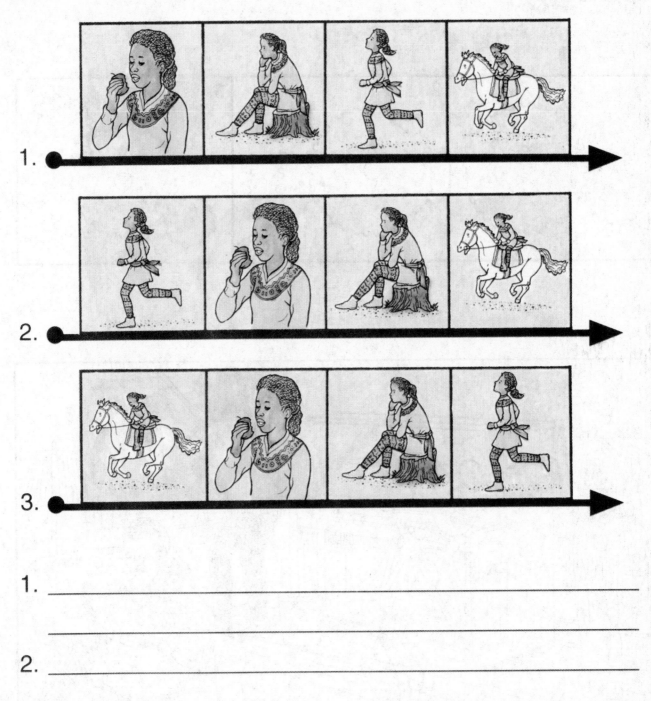

1. _____

_____

2. _____

_____

Lesson 58

A.

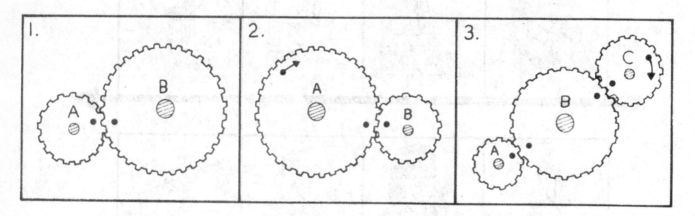

B.

washed	mopped	read	painted	book
	window	floor	piano	

C.

A.

1.	2.	3.
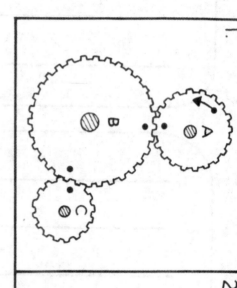	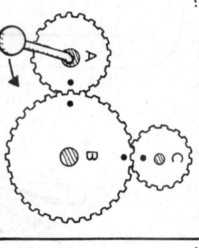	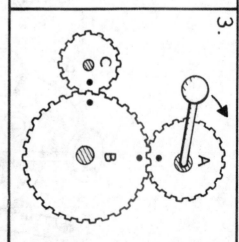

B.

The woolly worm goes 3 inches each second.
The spider goes 2 inches each second.

a. woolly worm   spider   d. ____   f. ____
b. woolly worm   spider   e. ____   g. ____
c. woolly worm   spider

FINISH

C.

rode   ate   played   jumped   read   rope

banana   book   violin   bike

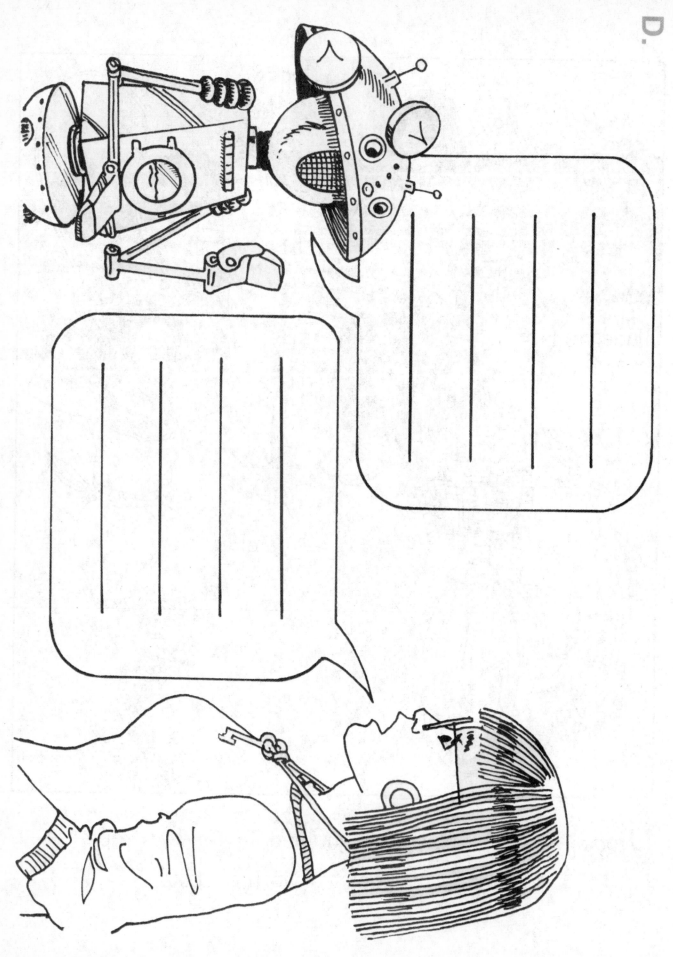

striped | bike | rode | patch | pants | small | shirt | wore

Test 6

A.

can   cake   corn   rat   tack   bend

B.

Bleep, come and help me.

1. Bleep was holding a can of paint.   reports   does not report

2. Only part of the fence was painted.   reports   does not report

3. Bleep did not hear Molly.   reports   does not report

4. Molly is getting irritated with Bleep.   reports   does not report

5. Molly's car door was open.   reports   does not report

6. Molly called for Bleep's help.   reports   does not report

C.

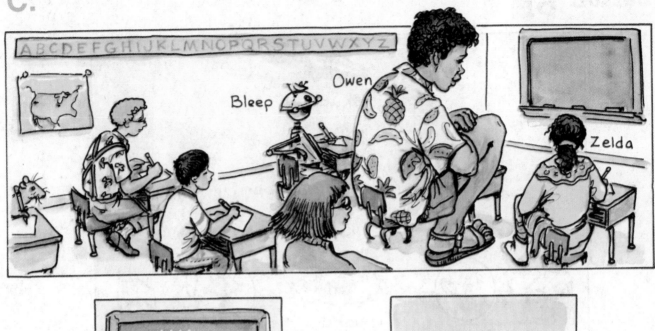

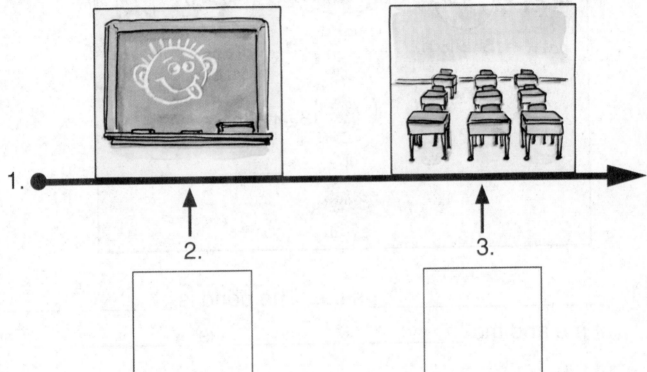

1.

2.

3.

A. The character who drew on the board is sitting in the front row.

B. _____

_____

C. _____

_____

Lesson 61

A.

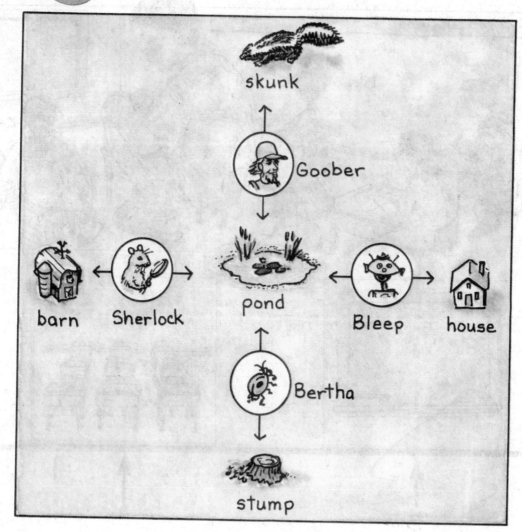

1. _____ said, "The pond is _____ of me and the _____ is _____ of me."

2. _____ said, "The pond is _____ of me and the _____ is _____ of me."

3. _____ said, "The pond is _____ of me and the _____ is _____ of me."

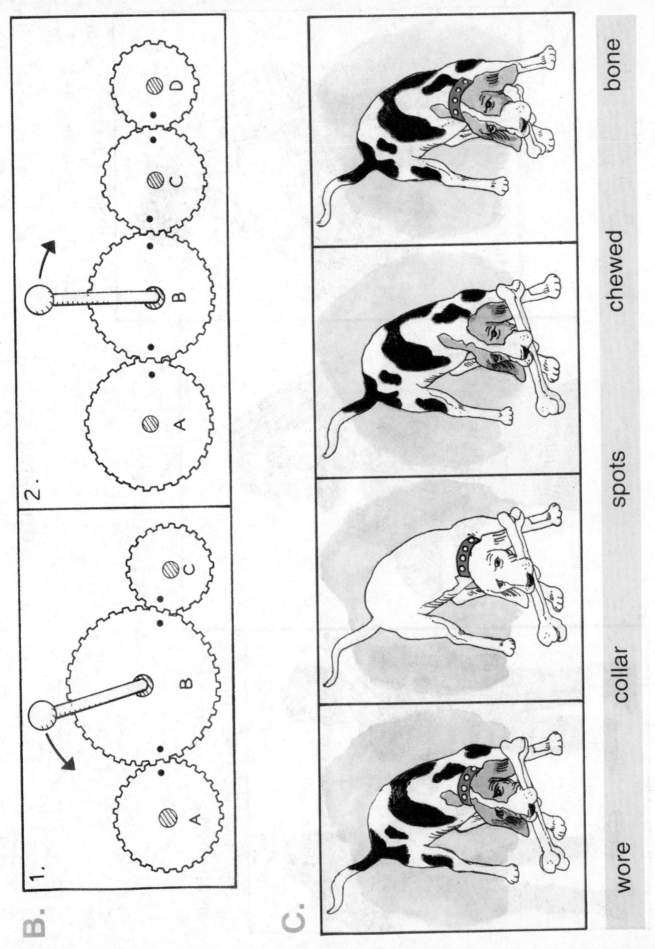

B.

1.

2.

C.

wore   collar   spots   chewed   bone

D.

It Folds Up

It was regular sized with two full-sized wheels.

Molly Henderson

Then it folded up to the size of a book.

She said, "I got the idea when I talked to him."

Angelo

accordion

FINISH

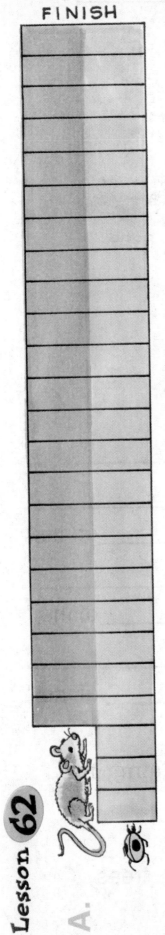

A.

a. Bertha ____ Sherlock
b. Bertha ____ Sherlock
c. Bertha ____ Sherlock

d. ____ Sherlock
e. ____ Sherlock
f. Bertha ____ Sherlock

g. ____
h. ____
i. ____

B.

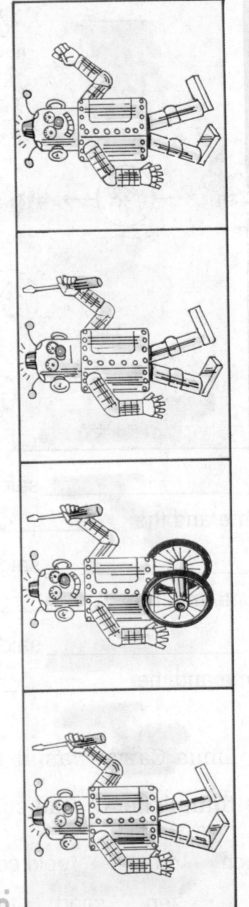

legs   wheels   smiled   held   screwdriver

C.

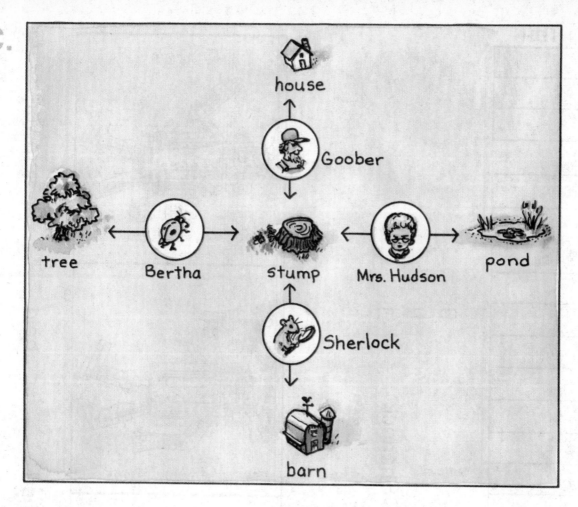

1. _____ said, "The stump is _____
   of me and the _____ is _____ of me."

2. _____ said, "The stump is _____
   of me and the _____ is _____ of me."

3. _____ said, "The stump is _____
   of me and the _____ is _____ of me."

D.

Linda Carry was at it. She was digging in it.

She found them. She sold them.

beach	rooster	gold coins	bushes	trees
	ten	sand	turkeys	money

A.

1. Mrs. Hudson rode her bike.

2. Mrs. Hudson _____

3. Mrs. Hudson _____

she   took   house   shower   after

B.

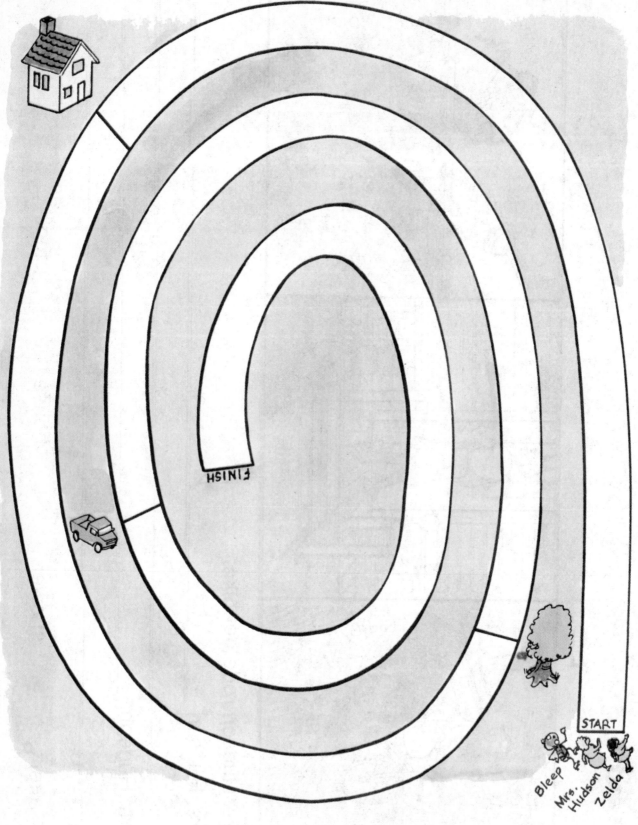

FINISH

START

Bleep

Mrs. Hudson

Zelda

1. _____   2. _____

3. _____   4. _____

C.

hair   glasses   smiled   long   wore

D.

E.

F.

1. B is not the safe landing place because B is not

   _____.

2. C is not the safe landing place because C is not

   _____.

Lesson 64

A.

Bleep goes 2 miles an hour.
Goober goes 3 miles an hour.

1. _____

2. _____

3. _____

4. at the _____

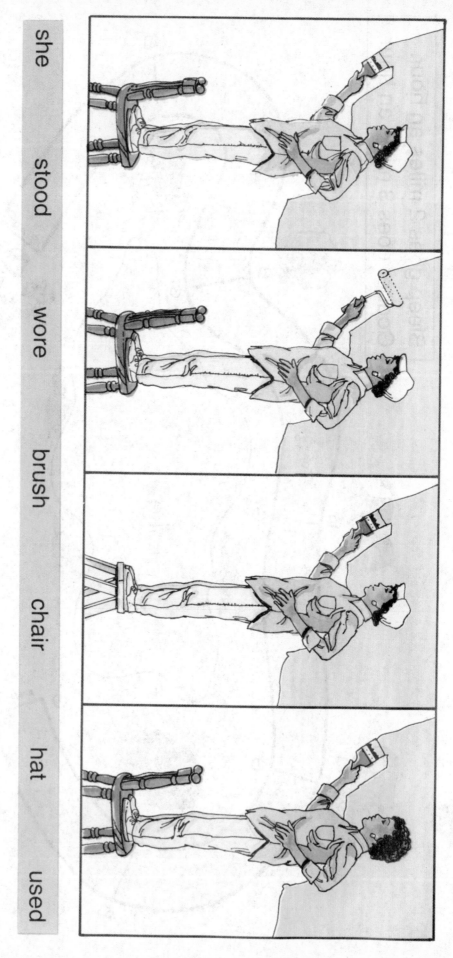

she   stood   wore   brush   chair   hat   used

C.

Map A

leaf

stick

Map B

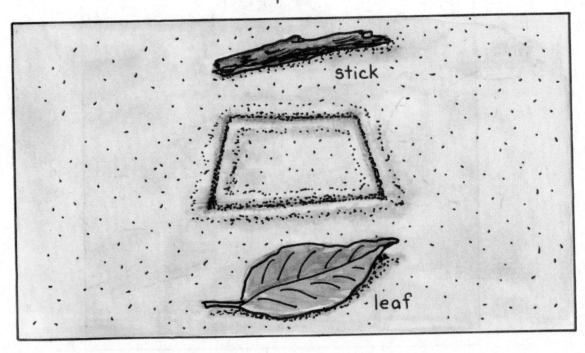

stick

leaf

D.

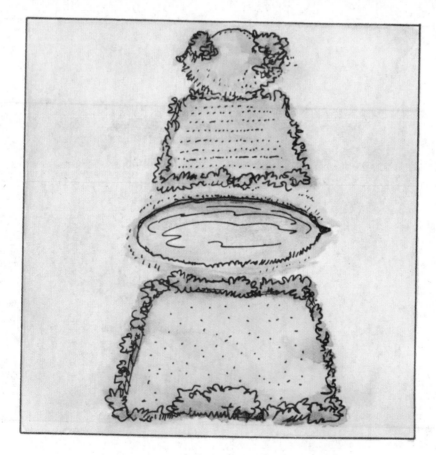

Lesson 65

A.

1. The girls planted trees. The trees were covered with green leaves.

2. The ladder was next to the house. The house had three windows.

3. Bleep saw Goober. Goober was shaving.

B.

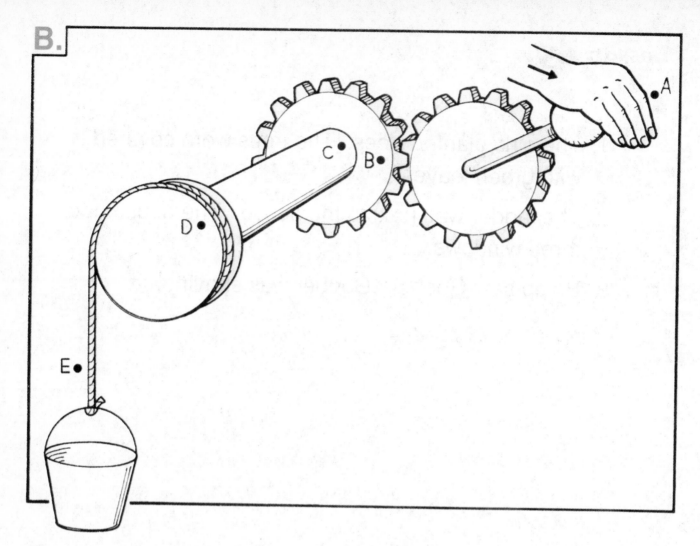

C.

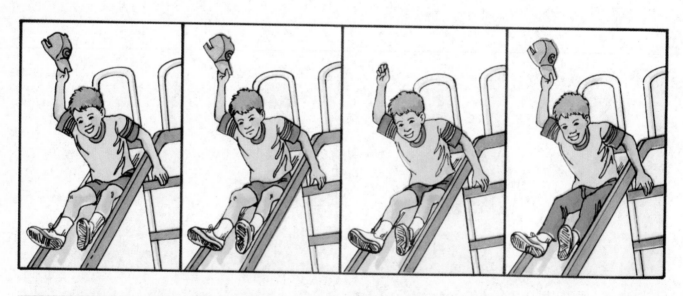

slid   slide   down   boy   shorts

smiled   held

D.

A.

1. Sherlock	a mouse	2. Sherlock	Bertha
3. Bleep	Roger	4. Molly	Bleep

B.

boots   coat   hook   went   door   inside

closed   took   off   hung   put   hat

C.

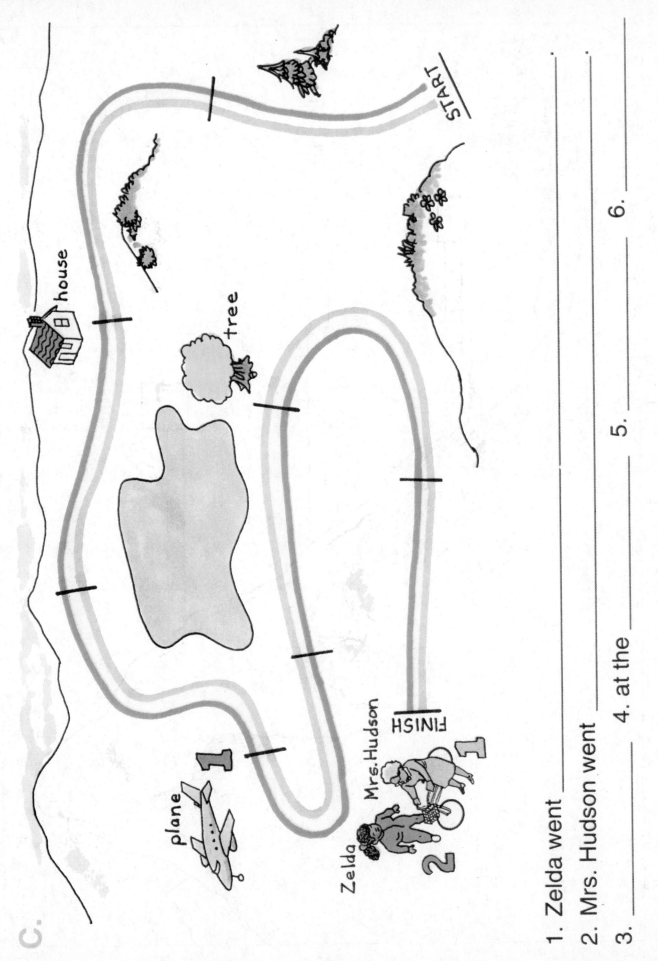

1. Zelda went _____

2. Mrs. Hudson went _____

3. _____

4. at the _____

5. _____

6. _____

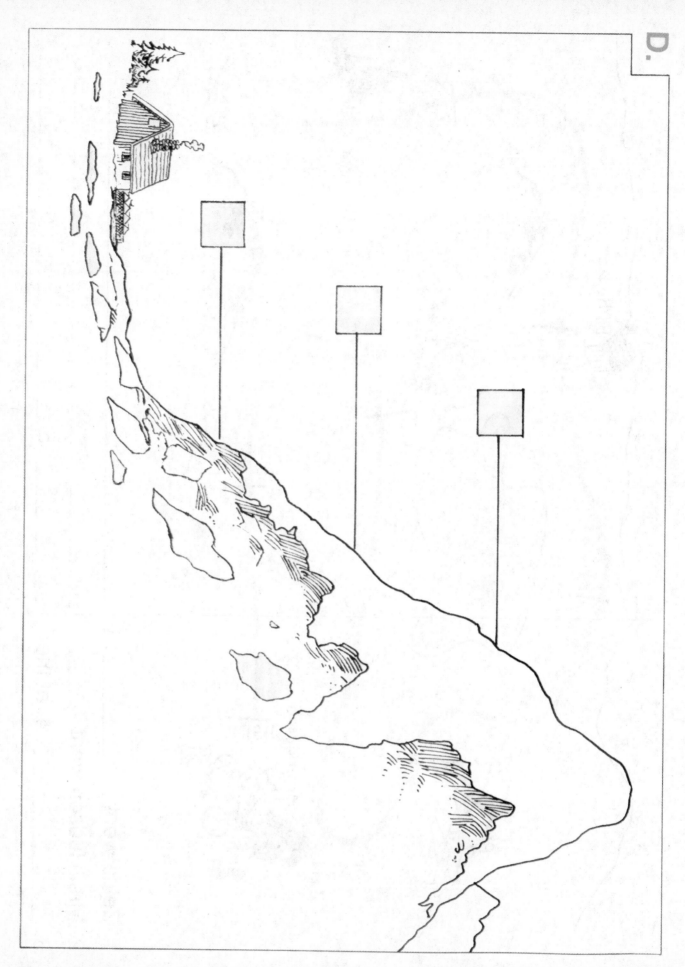

Lesson 67

A.

1.

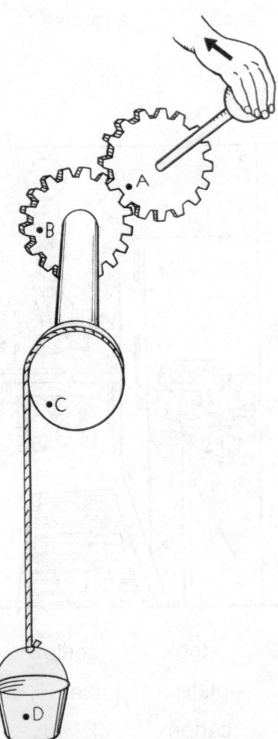

2.

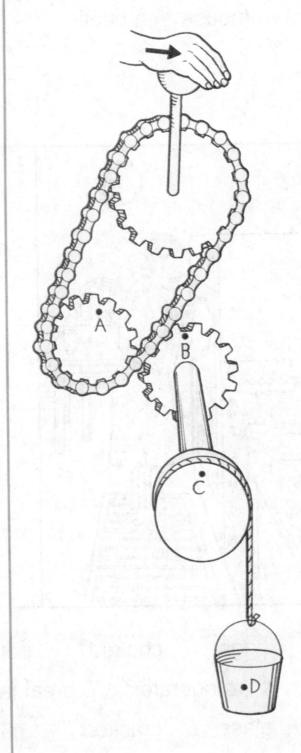

1. Molly   Zelda   2. Sherlock   Mrs. Hudson

3. a mouse   a beetle   4. a cat   a mouse

C.

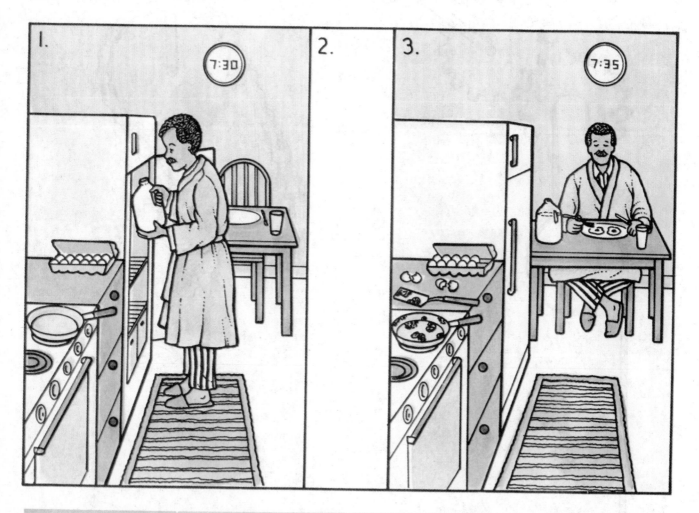

eggs	cooked	poured	took	bottle
refrigerator		breakfast	plate	table
glass	cracked	milk	carton	closed

E.

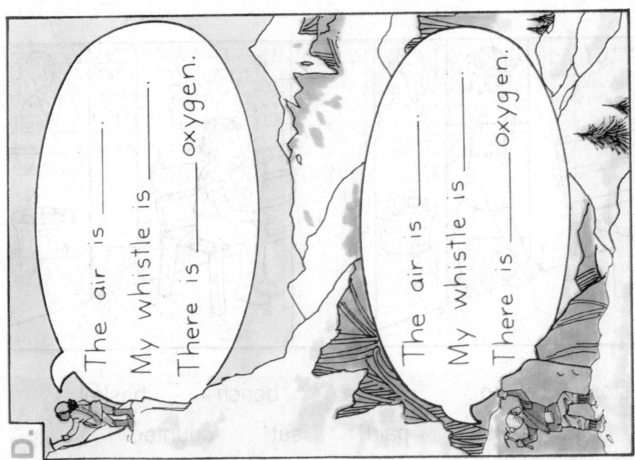

D.

The air is _____.

My whistle is _____.

There is _____ oxygen.

The air is _____.

My whistle is _____.

There is _____ oxygen.

Lesson 68

A.

jumped	water	held	cap
swim fins	nose	wore	pool

B.

store	into	outside	bench	basket
apples	paid	sat	counter	

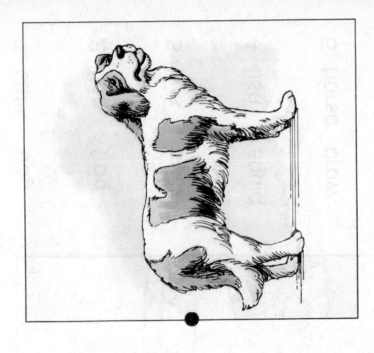

C.

I can't stand the cold.

I can run very fast on ground.

I can spend all day in the snow without getting very cold.

I have a very warm coat of fur.

My paws are small and I can't move well in snow.

Lesson 69

A.

1. cat   dog

2. dog   frog

3. bus   truck

4. fish   squid

5. horse   crow

B.

1.   2.   3.

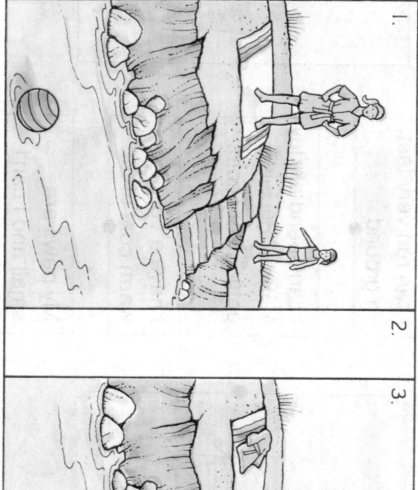

water	bank	stairs	beach ball	robe
blanket	jumped	swam	climbed	carried

C.

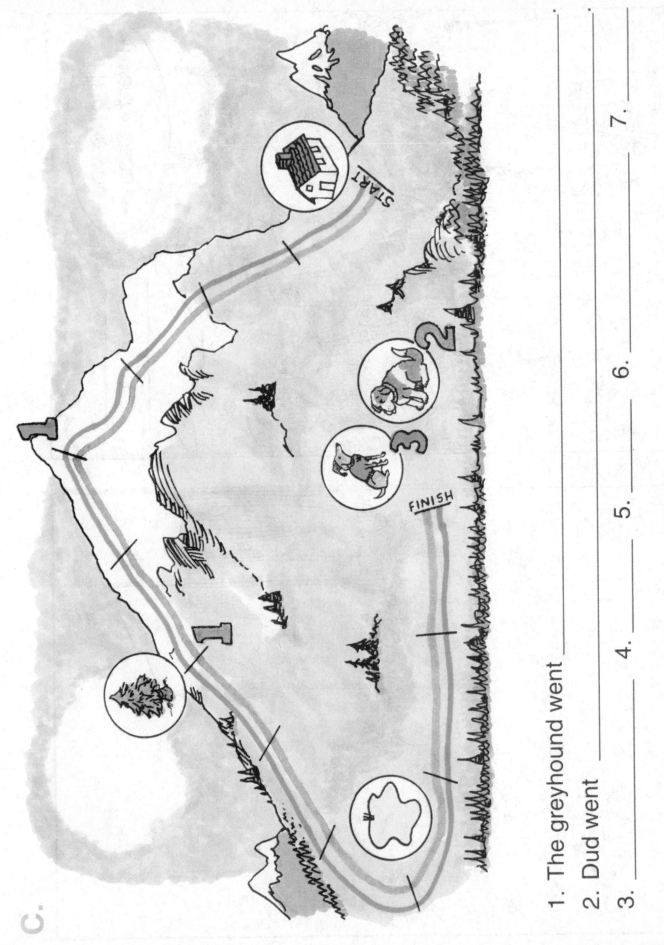

1. The greyhound went _____

2. Dud went _____

3. _____

4. _____

5. _____

6. _____

7. _____

D.

E.

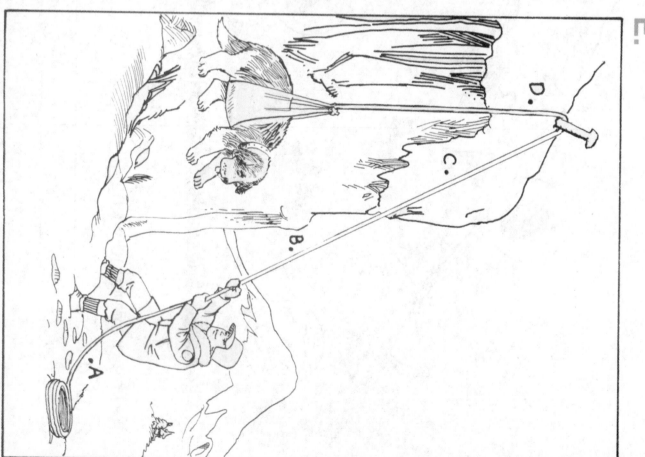

A.

1. Dooly   Horace

2. Dooly   Caw-Caw

3. Dooly   an eagle

B.

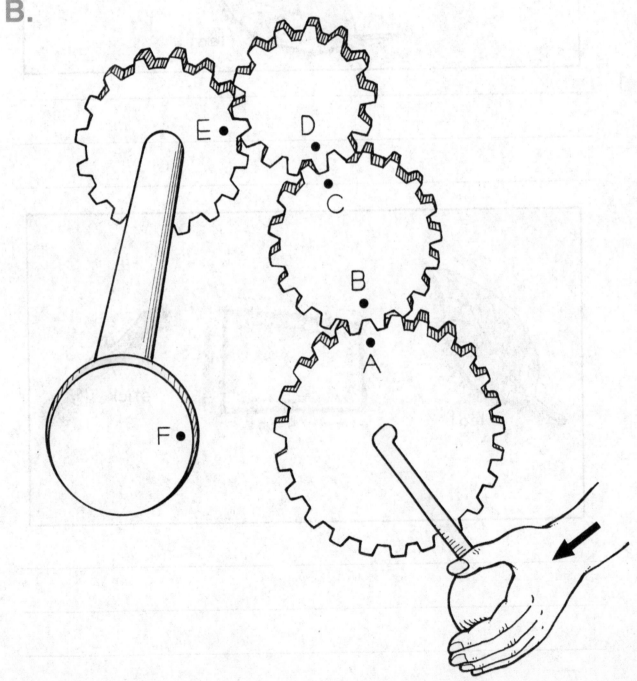

C.

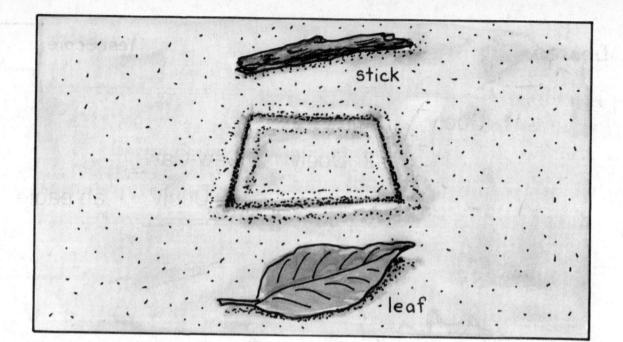

1. _____

_____

_____

2. _____

_____

_____

Extra Activities

A. Story Writing

1. _____ Dessera

2. _____ Dot and Dud

3. _____ Dooly

4. _____ Sherlock

5. _____ Zelda and Mrs. Hudson

6. _____ Owen, Fizz and Liz

7. _____ _____

B. Plays

1. _____ Dot and Dud with the Greyhounds

2. _____ Mrs. Hudson and Zelda

3. _____ Dooly and Caw-Caw

4. _____ Bleep and Molly

5. _____ Owen Visiting Fizz and Liz

6. _____ _____

C. Books

1. _____ A book by Mrs. Hudson and Zelda

2. _____ Letters sent to Owen and Fizz and Liz

3. _____ A book of silly Bleep-talk

4. _____ _____

D. Maps

1. _____ Our school

2. _____ Our neighborhood

3. _____ Our classroom

4. _____ _____

Dessera's Route